Take my
Plastic

Peter Maiden

Copyright © Peter Maiden 1997
First published in the UK 1997 by OM Publishing

03 02 01 00 99 98 97   7 6 5 4 3 2 1

OM Publishing is an imprint of Paternoster Publishing,
P.O. Box 300, Carlisle, Cumbria, CA3 0QS, U.K.

British Library Cataloguing in Publication Data

A catalogue record for this book is available from the British Library

ISBN 1-85078-263-6

Pierce my ear by S. Croft {Permission still to be obtained}
Mind over matter by Ranulph Fiennes {Permission still to be obtained}
The message {Permission still to be obtained}

Typeset by WestKey Ltd., Falmouth, Cornwall
Printed in the UK by Mackays of Chatham Plc.

Take my Plastic

Christian giving and stewardship for today

Peter Maiden

OM
publishing

Contents

Chapter 1

The Character of God
— the Foundation

I recently celebrated with my son his eighteenth birthday. We went go-carting. Twenty five laps for ten pounds! Not very good stewardship you might think but we had a great time.

The further I went through those twenty five laps the faster I got. I began to understand more and more what the little machine was capable of and probably what I was capable of! Corners were taken more quickly because I was beginning to understand that go-carts don't slide too easily. I began to see what the brakes could do. Increasing knowledge affected what I did.

I acquired the knowledge, which affected my actions in two ways. The twenty-five laps were preceded by some brief instructions from one of the staff and I also gained knowledge through experience.

I'm convinced that the knowledge of God gained through the instruction of his word and the reality of our experience of him will together impact what we do in our lives. There is *nothing* more important to us than our understanding of God. William Carey was sure that if we came to 'expect great things from God' we would 'attempt great things for' him. The greatest stimulus to holiness in our lives is an understanding of his holiness. 'Be holy because I am holy' (1 Peter 1:16) As we understand the love and faithfulness of God the selfishness and fear that dominate our lives will be replaced by carefree extravagant generosity.

The most important statement in Scripture related to giving is probably the best known. 'God so loved the world that he gave his only son' (John 3:16). God is a giving God. There must be something special about *3:16* because 1 John 3:16 contains an equally vital example and challenge. 'This is how we know what love is: Jesus Christ laid down his life for us.' Jesus is the Saviour who gave everything.

I remember how when our children were much younger we went through a particularly hard financial time. When they came asking for money I tried to respond but I was very careful to give only the exact amount they would require. That was so different from the way God gives to us. His generosity can be seen in creation.

'The Lord God made all kinds of trees grow out of the ground, trees that were pleasing to the eye and good for food' (Genesis 2:9).

The land that God gave to his people Israel was a land 'flowing with milk and honey' (Numbers 14:8).

The life that Jesus came to this earth to obtain for us is an abundant life — 'a life to be lived to the full' (John 10:10). The salvation we have in Jesus is not 'by the skin of our teeth,' 'since he is able to save completely those who come to God through him' (Hebrews 7:25). Paul reckoned it was impossible to grasp all the extravagance that God has prepared for his people. 'No eye has seen, no ear has heard, no mind has conceived what God has prepared for those who love him' (1 Corinthians 2:9).

If we are to live aright we have to understand that this is our God. He loves us, he is constantly giving extravagantly to us. He has the power to do so constantly. Our challenge is to be 'imitators of God' and to 'live a life of love just as Christ loved us and gave himself for us as a fragrant offering and sacrifice to God' (Ephesians 5:1,2). Imitate God, and live just as Christ lived, loving and giving himself.

Chapter 2

Stewardship

In the opening chapter I suggested that some people might not consider twenty-five laps of go-karting for ten pounds to be 'good stewardship'. A strange statement, you may think. Surely stewardship involves the management of resources that belong to someone else? Surely the ten pounds was mine? So what I did with it was my own business.

A second fundamental understanding that will impact what we do in our lives is the *biblical* concept of stewardship.

People often describe sports personalities or speakers as 'talented'. Such statements originate in a parable Jesus told. A man was going on a journey. As he left he gave five 'talents' to one of his servants, two to another and one to a third. A talent at the time of Jesus was a considerable sum of money. In his absence the first and second servants put their talents to work and made one hundred per cent profit, to the delight of their master. The third servant buried his solitary talent to keep it safe. Interestingly, it was his opinion of his master's character that motivated this action. 'I know', he said, 'that you are a hard man.' The one talent was taken from him and given to the servant who had ten.

Jesus, who is our master, has given everyone of his servants talents. He expects us to use them to advance his interests in this world.

The talents he gives us are much more than sums of money. All that we are and have, the spiritual and natural 'gifts' that we are given, all that we accumulate during our lifetime are to be dedicated not to the creation of a personal empire but to the advancing of his kingdom in this world.

This is at the very heart of Christian experience. For many of us it contrasts strongly with the way we used to live, summed up in such mottos as:

'Every man for himself.'
'Look after number one.'
'It's the survival of the fittest.'
'Do unto others before they do it unto you.'

The redemption of Jesus releases us from this slavery of serving ourselves and frees us to serve God and our fellow men and women.

Talking of slavery, there's an interesting law about it in Exodus 21:1-6. Hebrew servants could be bought by their master to serve for six years but in the seventh year they had to be freed without charge. Some apparently chose not to claim their freedom. Their relationship with their master was such that they wanted to continue in his service. A strange ceremony was then enacted. The master first took the servant before the judges, possibly to get an independent assessment that the servant really wanted to remain. Then 'he shall take him to the door or the door post and pierce his ear with an awl. Then he will be his servant for life.'

Some people think that Psalm 40:6 refers to this law. It reminds them of how Jesus was the willing servant of his father. 'Sacrifice and offering you did not desire but my ear you have pierced.' It also gives a picture of how a Christian may respond to Jesus. This is the thought behind S. Croft's song:

Pierce my ear O Lord my God,
Take me to your throne this day.
I will serve no other God,
Lord I'm here to stay.
For you have paid the price for me,
with your blood you ransomed me,
I will serve you eternally,
a free man I'll never be.

The earliest Christian confession of faith was
the three words, 'Jesus is Lord.' The word they
used for 'Lord' was 'Kyrios'. Donald Guthrie
explains that this was 'a title of respect in the
world of the New Testament, often used to
address the Roman emperor'. For Jews it had
particular significance in that they linked it
with the Hebrew word 'Adonai' which in turn
was often used as a substitute for Yahweh. In
the Christian use it implied the absolute sover-
eignty of Jesus over all aspects of faith and life.
He had become Lord and master and his followers willing bond slaves.

I own a home and a car amongst other things.
Acts 5:4 makes it clear that Christians have the
right to own possessions. However 'I love my
Master' and I want to dedicate these, along with
everything else which is mine, to further his

interests in this world. He is my sovereign. Jesus rules O.K.!

This is what stewardship means in a Christian context.

Chapter 3

'Gaining What You Cannot Lose'

Jim Elliot was one of five missionaries who were speared to death as they sought to take the good news of Jesus to the Auca Indians of Ecuador in January 1956. He is known to many today for something he wrote in his diary. 'He is no fool who gives what he cannot keep to gain what he cannot lose.' This sounds like a commentary on some words of Jesus: 'Whoever finds his life will lose it, and whoever loses his life for my sake will find it' (Matthew 10:39).

When did Jesus say this? If you look at Matthew 10 you will find that it's a tough chapter. Jesus is about to send out the twelve disciples on mission, so he explains some of the hardships they will face and the sacrifices that will be called for. This is why each of them needs to face the possibility of losing 'his life'.

It is vital to realise that when following and serving Christ means being called to sacrifice, then the apparent loss is actually gain. This was one of the points where some religious people in Jesus' day got it all wrong. Matthew 6 contains a picture of how the Pharisees practised prayer and fasting. They chose the most public place (v. 5) and put on the 'poor me' look and would actually whiten their faces in order to really tug at people's heart strings. But the message of Jesus was the exact opposite. If for any reason we have to endure difficulties in his name we shouldn't be thinking 'poor me'. Sacrifice should not leave us feeling sorry for ourselves or others feeling sorry for us.

Self-sacrifice need not involve self pity. In *Mind over Matter* Ranulph Fiennes describes his and Mike Stroud's attempt to make the first unassisted crossing of the Antarctic continent. The suffering they endured to achieve this was incredible. Fiennes recalls how, towards the end of the journey, Stroud

. . . slowed down until, some five hours into the day, he came to a complete halt with his head drooping forwards. Recognising the signs of imminent hypothermia I grew fearful and erected the tent immediately, for there was no wind. Mike's lisping attempts to talk were inaudible. He sat listlessly on his sledge and I asked him in a loud voice to collect snow for tea. He hit the plastic shovel against one of his fingers and whimpered with pain.

They have gone almost beyond the limits of endurance. They are totally exhausted. But nowhere do you detect a 'poor me' attitude. The book makes it clear that this is what they chose to do, this is what they wanted to do, they considered it a privilege to be where they were and to be doing what they were doing. They had a goal which had filled their minds for years and to sacrifice to achieve that goal was privilege.

In *The Grace of Giving*, Stephen Olford relates a story which Dr. Roy L. Laurin tells of a Christian businessman who was travelling in Korea. In a field by the side of the road was a young man pulling a simple plough while an old man held the handles. The business man was amused and took a snapshot of the scene. 'That is curious! I suppose these people are very poor', he said to the missionary who was interpreter and guide to the party.

'Yes', was the quiet reply, 'those two men happen to be Christians. When their church was being built, they were eager to give something toward it; but they had no money. So they decided to sell their one and only ox and give the proceeds to the church. This spring they are pulling the plough themselves.' The business man was silent for moments.

Then he said, 'That must have been a real sacrifice.'

'They did not call it that', said the missionary, 'they thought themselves fortunate that they had an ox to sell!'

When the business man reached home he took the picture to his pastor and told him the story. Then he added, 'I want to double my giving to the church and do some "plough" work. Up until now I have never given God anything that involved real sacrifice.'

Jesus told a story (Matthew 13:44) about a labourer who discovered buried treasure when he was digging in a field. In order to claim legal ownership of the treasure he must own the field. He thought no sacrifice too great in order to become the owner. 'He sold all he had.' You can imagine that friends and neighbours began to feel concerned for him. Had he fallen into serious difficulties? Was he mentally unwell? Any feelings of sorrow would vanish when as the owner of the field he claimed the treasure. Rather than seeking to console him for the sacrifices he had had to make you would want to congratulate him, and admire his sensible behaviour.

Jesus told the story to illustrate how entering the kingdom of heaven is such a treasure that we must be willing to surrender everything which would hinder us from achieving this. I don't think it is stretching the story too far to say that for Christians the privilege of pleasing Christ and of finally hearing him saying, 'Well done, faithful servant' is such that the endurance of any difficulties for that goal is hardly to be defined as sacrifice.

So what is it that Jesus calls his followers to? We shall find out by looking briefly at Luke 14: 25–33. It refers to 'great crowds' following Jesus. The statistics stating the number of Christians in the world today make encouraging reading. A recent survey puts the number at a staggering 1,782,809,000. With such figures very much depends on our definition of a Christian. Some parts of the world remain spiritually barren but in others it is becoming fashionable to be 'a born again'. Reading Luke's account you get the impression that Jesus is uncomfortable with the size of the crowd. Do they realize what he is about? Have they begun to understand him? He confronts them with the terms of true Christian discipleship. I wonder, How many will have been packing their bags and were ready to leave him after this opening statement?

'If anyone comes to me and does not hate his father and mother, his wife and children, his brothers and sisters — yes even his own life — he cannot be my disciple' (v. 26).

What did Jesus mean? Can this be the 'gentle Jesus meek and mild' who taught us to love our enemies? Can he now be telling us to hate our parents and our families? Surely the point Jesus is making when he uses the word 'hate' is that our love for him must be second to none. Every other love in our lives must be in submission to our love for him. In *The Message*, Eugene Peterson translates this; 'Anyone who comes to me but refuses to let go of father, mother, spouse, children, brothers, sisters — yes even his own self! — can't be my disciple.'

Sometimes this call to 'let go' of family gets very real in the world of missions. In a leaflet entitled 'He will not forsake my children', Alice Taylor gives a vivid example. Alice and her husband

James were missionaries in the Chinese province of Horan. Their four children were students at the famous missionary school in Chefoo, Shantung Province, a thousand miles away. When the Japanese invaded China the Taylors were cut off and it was impossible to get to Chefoo. Alice and James had to run for their lives, but as they fled their thoughts were constantly in Chefoo. At first a few letters were exchanged but then came a silence, soon explained by the newspaper headlines.

'PEARL HARBOUR ATTACKED. U.S. ENTERS WAR.' Alice Taylor remembers her feelings:

As I absorbed the news I realised why there had been a long silence from the children. Chefoo had been in the Japanese line of attack.

'Oh dear God' I whispered, 'my children, my children . . .' I knelt beside the bed. Not even tears came at first, just wave after wave of anguish.

As the fear penetrated deeper, I remembered the horror stories of Nanking, where all the young women of that town had been brutally raped. And I thought of our beautiful Kathleen, beginning to blossom into womanhood . . .

Great gulping sobs wrenched my whole body. I lay there gripped by the stories we had heard from refugees — violent deaths, starvation, the conscription of young boys — children — to fight.

I thought of ten year old Jamie, so conscientious, so even tempered. 'What has happened to Jamie, Lord? Has someone put a gun in his hands? Ordered him to the front lines? To death?'

Mary and John so small and so helpless had always been inseparable. 'Merciful God!' I cried, 'Are they even alive?'

Kneeling there by the bed pleading with God, I knew without any doubt at all that I had no other hope but God. I reached out to him now completely. 'Please help my children, help them be alive please!' Then as if in a dream I drifted back to a time when I was a girl of sixteen in Wilkes-Barre, Pennsylvania. I pictured our minister Pa Ferguson, sitting there telling me words he had spoken years ago. 'Alice if you take care of things that are dear to God, he will take care of the things dear to you.' That was Pa Ferguson's translation of 'Seek ye first the kingdom of God and his righteousness; and all these things shall be added unto you' (Matthew 6:33).

In the stillness of the bedroom I pondered Pa Ferguson's words. Who were the dear ones to God? The Chinese to whom God had called me to minister. And who were the ones dear to me? My children.

I did not know whether my children were alive or dead: nevertheless a deep peace replaced my agony. This war had not changed God's promises. With that assurance I felt the aching weight of fear in my stomach lift.

'All right God', I said finally. 'John and Mary and Kathleen and James are in your care. With all my heart I believe you will guard them. I know that you will bring us back together, and until that day comes I promise I will put all my energy into your work. I promise.'

Alice Taylor learned to let go of her family out of love for Christ. We are commanded to love our spouses, our parents and our children, but family sacrifice can be a consequence of our love for Jesus.

Jesus also said that the way to find life is to lose it. His next challenge to the crowd (v. 27) under-lines that principle with a vivid illustration. Imagine the scene. You are going about your duties in a Palestinian town, when suddenly a hush descends. Looking around, you see in the distance a group of men struggling through the town, weighed down by the wooden beams they are carrying. Everyone knows where the men are going. This is their last journey. They are as good as dead. This, says Jesus, is what it means to follow him. This, in total contradiction of popular opinion, is the way to life. You must 'take up your cross'. You must die to the old way of living, the old motivations, ambitions, the old ways of spending your time and money. In Christ you are a new creation. Following Jesus does not mean receiving a pleasant addition to your old life. It means the end of your life and the beginning of something entirely new.

This challenge underlies the message with which Jesus began his ministry. 'The time has come', he said. 'The kingdom of God is near. *Repent* and believe the good news' (Mark 1:15). He told his disciples that this same message would be proclaimed throughout the world. '*Repentance* and forgiveness of sins will be preached in his name to all nations, beginning at Jerusalem' (Luke 24:47). It was also the climax of Peter's sermon on the day of Pentecost. When the people asked, 'What shall we do?' Peter replied, '*Repent* and be baptized every one of you in the name of Jesus Christ for the forgiveness of your sins. And you will receive the gift of the Holy Spirit' (Acts 2:38). Paul, summing up his ministry, tells the leaders of the church at Ephesus, 'I have declared both to Jews and Greeks that they must turn to God in *repentance* and have faith in our Lord Jesus' (Acts 20:21). *Repentance* is central to the Christian message. But what does the word mean? According to a Bible dictionary, '*Metanoia*, the Greek word normally translated repentance, refers basically to a change of mind. It consists in a radical transformation of thought, attitude, outlook and direction.'

The New Testament passages quoted above show that such a transformation is a condition of salvation. Rather than Jesus being a pleasant addition to your present life there must be this radical transformation. There will be grief about much that made up your life before conversion. You only have to read David's psalm of repentance (Psalm 51) to see how repentance involves grief and hatred of sin.

Jesus' third challenge left the crowd in no doubt that 'taking up the cross' would affect every part of their lives. 'In the same way', he said, 'any of you who does not give up everything that he has cannot be my disciple (v. 33).'

Does this mean that we are immediately to put house sale signs up and empty bank accounts? Possibly yes! That is what it meant for C. T. Studd. Born into a wealthy family he moved through Eton on to Cambridge. His exploits on the cricket field made him a household name. God called him to China and soon after his arrival there the news came that he had inherited £29,000 — a huge sum in the late 1880s.

How did Studd handle the bequest? He began by donating four lump sums. Five thousand pounds went to the evangelist D. L. Moody, with a request that he commence a work in Tirhoot, North India, an area with which Studd's father had been associated. Five thousand went to George Muller of Bristol to support his amazing work amongst orphans. Work amongst the poor of London benefited from another five thousand pounds. The last five thousand went to the Salvation Army in India.

Studd made out a further five cheques for a thousand pounds each. One went to General Booth of the Salvation Army, three to individuals who were involved in preaching the gospel and caring for the poor in London and Dublin, and one to Doctor Barnardo for his work among children.

He then gave money to the China Inland Mission so that when his financial affairs were finally settled only £3,400 remained. Within six months he met Priscilla Stewart, who was to become his wife. Because the Bible says that 'if anyone does not provide for his relatives, and especially for his immediate family, he has denied the faith and is worse than an unbeliever' (1 Timothy 5:8), he decided to give the money to his bride. Her conviction proved to be the same as his and they gave everything that remained to General Booth of the Salvation Army.

Each of us is required to 'give up everything' to follow him. As we saw in the previous chapter, when Jesus becomes your Lord you take your hands off your life and you invite him to take full control of you — all that you are and all that you have. This is how Eugene Peterson translates (14:33): 'Simply put, if you are not willing to take what is dearest to you, whether plans or people, and kiss it goodbye, you can't be my disciple.'

I wonder how many of the crowd remained after this explanation of what was involved in following Jesus. Jesus is not discouraging discipleship; but he doesn't want anyone following him without realising what they have let themselves in for. Nominalism is the greatest enemy the church has had to face throughout the centuries and still today. The two pictures which Jesus paints in 14:28–32 express a serious warning.

My wife is constantly telling me not to start DIY jobs in the home without sitting down and planning them but I almost invariably do. I hammer the first nail in before I am really sure how the job will finish. Jesus describes a man who starts building a tower without estimating the cost. He can't finish it and his half-built tower is open to ridicule. A similar danger threatens the king who is considering going to war with an army of ten thousand men against a force of twenty thousand. He needs to sit down and assess the situation; failing this he will probably find that with the war hardly begun he has to find an emissary to negotiate a truce.

Bible teachers have pointed out that while these two illustrations are similar there is a significant difference. The man who built the tower was under no compulsion. To build was his choice. But did the king have a choice? Was he being invaded? There are two questions we must ask about following Jesus. Can I afford to follow him? As we have seen this is something which impacts every part of your life. But the second question is, can I afford not too? Remember: 'Whoever finds his life will lose it, and whoever loses his life for my sake will find it' (Matthew 10:39).

Chapter 4

God wants more than your Covenant Form

We love our Lord. We choose to be his bond slaves. Our 'ears are pierced'. We have seen that the choice we have made demands of us all that we are and have. This book will concentrate on the demands discipleship makes, on our attitude to possessions. I realise there is a danger in this. To speak plainly, the church has suffered too long from the problem caused by those who are content to 'pay their dues'. Giving a little money may be no more than an attempt to salve your conscience. As a 'full time' Christian worker, and accepting the gifts that others give to me, I have really struggled in recent years with one person who gives to me regularly. He used to be a very committed follower of Christ but it is clear from his lifestyle that he is no longer. My problem is that when he gives to me I have the real impression that it makes him feel better. Does the commitment of his money make him feel better about the lack of commitment of his life?

The church at Corinth, has set later Christians a great example in giving. We will note their example on a number of occasions. But in his second letter to them Paul teaches them (and us) a very important lesson by referring to the churches in Macedonia, way to the north of Corinth. In 2 Corinthians 8:5, writing about their sacrificial giving for famine relief in Jerusalem, he says that 'they first gave themselves to the Lord and then to us by the will of God'. These Macedonian Christians were not just giving money. They were giving themselves to God and the giving of their money to his work and his people was an expression of that. God does not just want a weekly cheque from us or even a four-year covenant form, he wants us.

One of the world's richest men was on business in Paris when he remembered that it was his son's sixteenth birthday. He immediately rang his home in America and contacted his son. He felt guilty, he had been away so much. 'What do you want for your birthday?' he asked. 'You name it; you can have it.' Surely such an offer would make up for his many absences. He was devastated by his son's reply. 'Dad I want you.'

Many of us are familiar with the beautiful 'hymn of love' in 1 Corinthians 13. But is it possible to become so familiar with it that we miss its challenge? Paul is clear: 'You can give everything, go to the ultimate in self-sacrifice but you can do it all for yourself and not God.' Once we have given ourselves to God, we understand that what we possess isn't really ours, but God's.

These warnings are necessary. Yet I believe that, particularly at this time in the western world, what we do with our resources is a vital expression of our discipleship. With the acquisition of material things still the ruling motive in the lives of so many today, and with such staggering spiritual and physical needs all around us, the cheque book is as vital a test of our devotion as the hymn book.

Chapter 5

Giving in the Old Testament

As long as people have experienced the goodness and the salvation of God they have responded with voluntary sacrificial giving. Entrusted by God with making a new start in the world after the flood, Noah might have been expected to conserve his resources. But Noah's first priority on leaving the ark is to give of his best to God (Genesis 8:20). Even as early as Genesis 4:3 we find Cain and Abel bringing some of their produce to God as an offering. We have no record that God demanded this of them. It was a freewill offering.

Tithing

This grateful response to God's goodness by giving was given divine approval in the law. Tithing, a custom which was practised by a number of ancient peoples, became part of what God required from his people. In one sense tithing was not giving. The tithe belonged to God not to the people. 'All the tithe of the land, of the seed of the land or of the fruit of the tree, is the Lord's. It is holy to the Lord' (Leviticus 27:30).

How the Tithe should have been   Tithing was a beautiful religious principle. Verse 32 shows how the tithing of livestock took place. As the animals passed out to pasture the owner would give every tenth one to God. In this way there was no possibility of selecting the inferior ones to be given and keeping the best (v. 33). The laws governing tithing which God gave to his people are quite clear and uncomplicated. This was intended to be a generous, simple response from the people of God in recognition of his goodness to them.

What the Tithe became   To these comparatively simple laws religious leaders added one complication upon another until a beautiful religious practice became a burden which, rather than being a source of joy, weighed constantly upon the people and robbed them of their joy. Tithing also became for many an outward sign of religious performance when the reality was very different. Jesus rebuked the Pharisees: 'Woe to you teachers of the law and Pharisees, you hypocrites! You give a tenth of your spices — mint, dill and cummin. But you have neglected the more important matters of the law — justice, mercy and faithfulness. You *should* have practised the latter without neglecting the former' (Matthew 23:23). The hypocrisy was shameful and Jesus condemns it in the strongest terms but we notice that even in doing this he does not criticize their actual tithing.

Tithing Today?

I have often heard people say that 'tithing is not for today'. It was part of the law which Jesus fulfilled on our behalf and thus has no relevance for us today. However those who teach this would, when pressed, not argue that we should give less than the tithe today. Many would say if that was the amount expected 'under law' much more would be expected 'under grace'.

If that is what people believe, then do we even need to mention tithing as a principle for today? If there is agreement that we should give more, then why mention it? Yes, but there is one problem. If every Christian was giving a tenth I don't think there would be a church or mission organisation anywhere in the world with financial difficulties. This is not the case! Something is going adrift! The problem may be very simple. When tithing was widely practised in the church many Christians were both organized and meticulous. As a boy I remember 'the Lord's tin'. There were other tins in the home, not least the 'holiday tin', but ten per cent went into 'the Lord's tin' as regular as clockwork. Is it possible that some of us today talk very generous and genuinely believe we are being generous but if at the end of the day we did some calculating then we would find, possibly to our great surprise, that we are giving much less than ten per cent.

Others have a more fundamental problem. How can I contemplate giving ten per cent in these days of recession? I'm challenged to make ends meet with the full one hundred per cent. In effect, they are saying: 'I can't afford to tithe!'

The Bible presents an opposite view. You can't afford not to tithe! This is one very practical area where we can put God and his word to the test. This was how God challenged his people through Malachi: 'Bring the whole tithe into the storehouse that there may be food in my house. *Test me* in this says the Lord Almighty and see if I will not throw open the floodgates of heaven and pour out so much blessing that you will not have room enough for it' (Malachi 3:10). More than once Scripture makes this direct unmistakable link between obedient giving and spiritual blessing.

How many believers and churches have you met who say they are longing for more blessing?

I want to encourage you if you have not already done so to install tithing as a principle in your life. It was a principle which preceded the law given to Moses. Four hundred years before that law was given we find Abraham (Genesis 14), after winning a famous victory, giving a tenth of everything to that mysterious figure Melchizedek. It is clear that this is the grateful response of Abraham to God who he acknowledges has won this victory for him.

If tithing was not intended to be our practice today then Jesus ignored a wonderful opportunity to make that clear in his teaching. If you read Matthew 23:1–22 you will see that Jesus is pulling no punches in condemning much of the Pharisees'

behaviour. In verse 23 he mentions their tithing.
Here also he has words of condemnation: 'You
give a tenth of your herbs — mint, dill and cummin. But you have neglected the more important
matters of the law — justice, mercy and faithfulness.' Clearly Jesus believed certain aspects of the
law were more important than others and tithing
was not the most important. But it is also clear
that (as we have already mentioned) you may deal
correctly with your money while your life is in a
total shambles! How are the Pharisees to put
things right? Jesus continues: 'You should have
practised the latter without neglecting the former.'
As R. T. Kendall points out: 'If tithing was a part
of the law that would or could be dropped under
the new covenant this is the place our Lord would
have done it. He did not.'

The Blessings of Generosity

In addition to the tithe, which as we have seen was
considered to be the Lord's, God looked for a
generous spirit among his people. Generosity towards the poor was encouraged (Deuteronomy
15:7–8). The law of gleaning was a beautiful law
which allowed the poor, orphans and foreigners

to glean grain, grapes and olives. 'When you reap the harvest of your land, do not reap to the very edges of your field or gather the gleanings of your harvest. Do not go over your vineyard a second time or pick up the grapes that have fallen. Leave them for the poor and the alien. I am the Lord your God' (Leviticus 19:9–10).

On a number of occasions God shows through his prophets that his blessing on the nation is closely linked to their generosity, particularly towards the poor. We find a powerful example of this in Isaiah 58:1–12. It is clear from this passage that the Israelites were maintaining a public display of religion. They worshipped in the temple regularly. They fasted. But they were not 'dividing their bread with the hungry or bringing the homeless into their houses or clothing the naked'. God's promise was clear: if they changed their ways his blessing would come upon them. 'If you give yourself to the hungry, and satisfy the desire of the afflicted, then your light will rise in the darkness, and your gloom will become like midday' (v. 10).

Both as a nation and as individuals they could expect God's blessing if they practised generosity (Deuteronomy 15:6, 10).

We can see how things should be amongst God's people when we read what happened when

God instructed Moses to encourage the Israelites to bring their gifts in order to make a sanctuary. The offering was to come from 'all whose hearts prompt them to give' (Exodus 25:2). Exodus 36:5–7 describes how they brought more than enough and had to be restrained from bringing any more towards the work.

Give God what's Left!

If Exodus 25 is a picture of how it should be among the people of God then the prophecy of Malachi is a picture of how things can so easily become. The situation here is almost beyond belief. Rather than giving the firstfruits they were offering polluted food and blind animals on the altar. These were things they would never have presented to the Persian governor who ruled over them but they were perfectly ready to offer them to God (Malachi 1:18). But is it really difficult to believe that Israel could fall so low? Am I giving God the best of my time, first call on my resources? Or do I make sure that I am perfectly comfortable first and then, if there is anything left of my time or my money, consider giving to God as a possible option? Again God's word to Israel is perfectly clear. If they will stop robbing him and bring the whole tithe (3:10) then the windows of heaven will be opened and they will enjoy an overflowing blessing.

Chapter 6

The Blessings of Giving

Please read this chapter with your Bible open at 2 Corinthians 8. The first fifteen verses give some practical reasons why faithful giving will bring blessing to our lives.

It's easy to assume that the Christians in Corinth were all unsanctified and worldly. But there were some admirable believers in that church as well. Paul speaks well of them when he says, 'Just as you excel in everything — in faith, in speech, in knowledge, in complete earnestness and in your love for us — see that you also excel in this grace of giving' (2 Corinthians 8:7). He wants to see the Corinthians giving concrete practical expression to their faith.

How deep is your love?

Paul was very impressed by how the poor Christians in Macedonia responded to the emergency in Jerusalem. Macedonia was a region heavily taxed by the Romans. The Christians there had endured persecution almost from the day they had responded to the gospel, and that persecution would often include financial loss. They were a very poor group of Christians and their giving was both an example and a challenge to others. Now Paul writes, 'I want to test the sincerity of your love by comparing it with the earnestness of others'(v.8). Do you want to know your spiritual temperature? Clearly if you check your giving pattern this will give some indication of your spiritual health. It is a very quantifiable test, isn't it? The fervency of our worship is not as easily computed as our giving records. In effect, Paul is saying, 'I've seen the love of the Macedonians in the way that they responded to the believers in Jerusalem. Now I will be able to see your love in this very visible way by looking at your response to the same situation.' Jesus said that if you really want to know where your heart is, one test is to look at where your treasure is (Matthew 6:21). When you receive money, whether it's your pay packet or an inheritance or whatever, what is your first thought? Is it about feathering your own nest or about how the money could be used to advance your heavenly Father's interests in this world? Let's be honest. Our first thought will probably be of our own nests; we are fallen human beings. But do we battle against that? Do we refuse to allow the standards of this age to dominate our lives? Are we prepared to discipline ourselves to respond biblically? Love is not just an emotion. It is a choice, a decision of the will.

How much do you want to grow?

Paul is sure that it is best for the Christians at Corinth if they give (v. 10). In the next chapter he develops this thought. If they sow sparingly they will reap sparingly but if they sow generously they will reap generously (2 Corinthians 9:6). Do you want spiritual blessing? Do you want just a little or a generous amount? We know that merely giving does not guarantee God's blessing. We have already seen that giving can be a conscience soother for people who are holding back from giving their lives. But Paul's statements here make it clear that you cannot separate spiritual growth from generous giving.

One of the most important learning experiences in my own life took place in Spain, on a main road in Valencia. I was on an evangelistic team there in the early days of O.M. (Operation Mobilisation). Things were not quite 'all together' at that stage! It was the third day in the city. The team leader from Mexico came up to me in the street to tell me that we had run out of money. I was just expressing my surprise, as this was only the third day of a three-month mission, when he further informed me that we had run out of food. Feeling immediately hungry I enquired what the plan was. He said, 'We are going to get on our knees here and remind God of his promises.' It wasn't quite the done thing back in my home city to drop to your knees in the main street but before I could stop him he was down! I felt an obligation to kneel beside him. I will never forget this man repeating the words of Philippians 4:19 in broken English 'My God will meet all your needs according to his glorious riches in Christ Jesus.' Suddenly it was crisis point in my life. I had been brought up to believe this book and to believe that God was faithful to his promises. But I had never been in a position like this! This was for real. Well I am still here, God was true to his word and I learned some very special lessons on a street in Valencia in a very brief space of time.

Most of us find it extremely difficult not to become dependent on the things that we possess. Our peace in the present and our confidence for the future quickly become more dependent on our possessions than the promises of God. I believe just one area where spiritual growth will result as we adopt a more radical sacrificial approach to giving is in the realm of trust in God.

What do you really believe?

We have already noted that the Corinthians excelled in everything — in faith, in speech, in knowledge, in complete earnestness and in love for Paul and his companions (v. 7). But would their beliefs impact their lives, the decisions and choices they made? The choices we make about the use of our resources are a very eloquent statement of our beliefs. Some years ago, when I was still quite young, I used to visit a man and his wife. They lived in a small mansion, just the two of them in this barn of a place, surrounded by antique furniture, and, standing in the driveway, a number of cars from which they could choose. His constant topic of conversation was the imminence of the second coming of Christ and he would regularly remind me that we were just pilgrims and sojourners passing through this world. I remember thinking on a number of occasions, 'If this is camping, I'm all for it.'

Do we really believe in heaven? Are we convinced that heavenly treasure is indestructible whereas treasure stored on earth is prone to destruction by moth and rust? In his epistle James writes of rich oppressors who were 'hoarding wealth in the last days' (James 5:3). James warns that their wealth would add fuel to the fire of God's judgment upon them on that last day. This judgment would not be because they were rich but because they were using their riches to oppress rather than serve and because they were hoarding. And as they hoarded their wealth so it was corroding. In addition to their sin of oppression they were guilty of waste. God does not give Christians wealth in order for them to hoard it. Wealth is for use. It is given, just like spiritual gifts, for service. If we serve faithfully with the resources we are given rather than using our wealth to add fuel to the fire of God's judgment, it can be the foundation for our future (1 Timothy 6:19).

In his book, *Joy in Ministry*, Michael Duduit tells the story of J.C. Stribling and the 1929 stock market crash in America. Prior to the depression Stribling was a wealthy Texas rancher. He owned a great deal of land, thousands of head of cattle, and a fortune in stocks and bonds. During this time he gave $150,000 to build a girls' dormitory on the campus of Mary Hardin-Baylor college, a Baptist college in Texas.

Then came the depression. Stribling lost his entire fortune. He was reduced to virtual poverty.

One day in 1933 a man came to the side of Stribling's old, run down Ford, and spoke to Stribling and his wife. Pastor Brandon explained that he had just returned from driving a group of girls to enrol at the college. He had spent the night there and now wanted to thank Mr. Stribling for his gift to the college. Stribling was silent for a few moments as his eyes filled with tears. Then he spoke: 'That was all we saved out of a mighty fortune. It was what we gave away that we were able to keep for ever.'

Then he added this challenge: 'Preacher, tell people to give all they can to the kingdom of God while they have it. I wish I had given more.'

Can it ever be fair?

The television has brought the suffering of the developing world right into our front rooms. Pop stars and comedians have compelled us to consider our responsibilities. Groups such as Tear Fund and World Vision have helped many Christians to think through the issue of how we should respond to poverty and have given reliable channels for us to give money with confidence. We have seen how a famine caused urgent need in first-century Jerusalem. Although Paul urged the Corinthians to give, he didn't want to see one need met by creating another (vv. 13, 14). 'Our desire is not that others might be relieved while you are hard pressed but that there might be equality.' Paul envisages a giving and taking among Christians. 'At the present time your plenty will supply what they need, so that in turn their plenty will supply what you need. Then there will be equality.'

God disapproves when some Christians are in the lap of luxury and others have barely enough to live. But how can we apply this truth to our situation today? The most common response to the pictures of the hungry is still apathy. This is not because we have no feelings but because we feel that the little we can do is not going to make any difference.

If we are to live biblically we cannot allow ourselves the luxury of thinking like that. On a number of occasions the Bible teaches us that when we are alerted to need and are able to help, then we must do so, and with actions not just words, otherwise we are denying the faith we profess (1 John 3:17). The fact is, we are able to help. *You* can make a difference. My home church has been supporting the building of a hospital in Bombay, India where the poor will be treated for little or no charge. In our family service we began the practice of giving tubes of 'Smarties' to the children, encouraging them to bring the tubes back the following week full of coins. It seemed such a small amount, and the project so large by comparison. Week by week the tubes have come back, and in fact continue to come. Hundreds of pounds have now been raised through this method for this hospital which opened its doors to patients just a few weeks ago.

It is not just the giving of money which will redress this inbalance in our world. The director of that hospital in Bombay was following a successful medical career in the U.K. when the call to the poor in his homeland of India came to him loud and clear. He and his newly married bride faced some tough decisions and a total change of lifestyle. Now that hospital can use medical staff from other parts of the world who are willing to leave their own work for a few months and serve there in a voluntary capacity.

Recent initiatives by the Evangelical Alliance and Tear Fund have been showing us that poverty is not a thousand miles away. They have launched U.K. Action, which they describe as a £10 million campaign to help ease the plight of poor people in Britain. They will finance community development projects run by local churches, to support the socially deprived, such as isolated elderly people and those who are long – term unemployed.

This raises the question of appropriate lifestyle. And it's a thorny question. What should be our lifestyle, in the light of the enormous spiritual and physical needs with which we are surrounded. It is such a vital matter that we shall devote chapter 9 to it. But this is a good point to encourage ourselves with 2 Corinthians 9:8. Paul has appealed to the Corinthians to give generously (v. 6), freely and cheerfully (v. 7). Then he promises: 'and God is able to make it up to you by giving you everything that you need and more so that there will be not only enough for your own needs but plenty left over to give joyfully to others' (v. 8 – *Living Bible*).

Apparently Paul is not the only one who doesn't want to ease problems by creating others. That is also God's way. If we are prepared to give generously, freely and cheerfully, then God will give to

us. How much? 'Everything you need and more.'
But why 'more'? Is it so that we might prosper?
No: we can use 'the left over . . . to give joyfully
to others'. Here is a chain reaction which will
release people from all kinds of chains. Be generous. When you are alerted to need and you have
the means respond generously, freely and with a
smile on your face. You will find that God will
respond to you and sometimes his response will
be to give you even more resources, which in turn
will enable you to be generous again.

What's in it for me?

I don't really like this question. I don't like it
because I believe if *that* becomes our motive we
are in deep trouble. As we have seen, our giving
must be a grateful response to God's goodness to
us. We give for his glory, to extend his work in
this world, not our own empires. This matter of
motive is so vital that the next two chapters will
concentrate on it.

And yet — although personal gain must not be
our motive, the Scriptures teach clearly that the
Christian giver can't lose. So let me for a moment
be your financial advisor.

First let me tell you how to place your resources in a deposit beyond any danger from the collapse of financial markets or banks, in a place where rogue traders cannot cause havoc. Jesus told us to 'store up for yourselves treasures in heaven, where moth and rust do not destroy, and where thieves do not break in and steal' (Matthew 6:19). Second, let me explain how your resources can definitely be a blessing rather than a burden to you. Jesus also said, 'It is more blessed to give than to receive' (Acts 20:35). The experience described by Michael Griffiths in his book, *Take My Life*, is typical of many:

> Our personal experience as a family has been that we have so far never been allowed to part with some substantial donation over and above our normal giving without it being abundantly returned from some other source and often multiplied into the bargain. So that, even down here, we seem to get our share of heavenly treasure too. God is no man's debtor. His giving to us (which is not to be measured merely on a financial scale) is always and evidently on a scale which makes our giving to him seem utterly puny by comparison.

This subject of giving is a vital one. I hope I have shown you some good reasons why you should take it very seriously.

Chapter 7

Cheerful Giving

As we stand in the streets of first-century Jerusalem we might almost be looking at the Salvation Army Band. In fact, it's a group of Pharisees. But why are they blowing trumpets? It seems they are trying to attract a crowd. Look at what they are doing now. Once the crowd has gathered, but only then, do they make their gifts to the poor. Jesus had just one thing to say about such people. 'If they give to be honoured by others they have received their reward in full' (Matthew 6:2).

The amount people are able to give will vary. The value to God is not in the amount. Remember the story of the widow, watched by Jesus and his disciples, who could only put two very small copper coins into the temple treasury. She was surrounded by rich people who were obviously putting in a lot more cash than she was. Yet Jesus' comment was. 'This poor widow has put in more than all the others' (Mark 14: 41–44). While the amount we are able to give will vary, the way we give should be the same whether we are giving a million or a mite!

The right motive

As we have already seen, we must give for the glory of God and to further his work in this world. Motive is vital. Paul pictures a man whose willingness to sacrifice is unquestionable. 'If I give all I possess to the poor and surrender my body to the flames . . .' But Paul points out that it is possible to do all that from an entirely wrong motive and for it to be an entirely profitless exercise (1 Corinthians 13:3).

Having recognized this danger, we should beware of motive paralysis! We must not get to the point where we spend so much time worrying whether our motive is correct that we never do anything. The example, already mentioned, of the Macedonians who gave themselves to the Lord as well as giving

their money for famine relief, is the best way to
ensure correct motive. If the giving is coming from
someone who is totally committed to the Lord Jesus
then that person's motive will not be to get anything
for self but everything for Jesus.

A practical outcome of this for many people is
anonymous giving. After pointing out the hypocrisy of the trumpet – blowing Pharisees, Jesus says,
'When you give to the needy, do not let your left
hand know what your right hand is doing, so that
your giving may be in secret. Then your Father
who sees what is done in secret, will reward you'
(Matthew 6:3, 4). John Stott suggests that this
instruction from Jesus is not intended only to
deliver us from telling the world about our giving.
He points out that it is the right hand that would
normally be used to hand over any gift. The fact
that Jesus says our left hand must not be watching
implies that we are not even to tell ourselves about
our giving. Self-conscious giving very quickly de-
teriorates into self-righteousness.

The right plan

Tom Rees, the evangelist, wrote in his book,
Money Talks, 'Regular disciplined giving is just as

important to spiritual development as regular worship, prayer and Bible study.' I trust you have a plan for your Bible reading and also a prayer diary or some equivalent. I pray that by the time you get to the end of this book you will be sitting down to work on your giving plan, if you have not already got one. It is clear that Paul expected the Corinthian Christians to have a systematic approach to giving. 'On the first day of every week, each one of you should set aside a sum of money in keeping with his income, saving it up, so that when I come no collections will have to be made' (1 Corinthians 16:2). On occasion you will hear of urgent needs and you will want to make an immediate response, but not all our giving should be like this. There will be people and projects that you have become linked with. You are familiar with them, sure of their value and credibility and these you will want to support in a regular systematic way. Bank standing orders and deeds of covenant help in systematizing our giving.

The right face

When we give there should be a smile on our face! After all, giving is not just a Christian duty. It is certainly not a burden which our religion places on us. It is a privilege.

As I write this, I recall a book on 'How to Develop a Tithing Church', mentioned by John MacArthur in his own *Giving God's Way*. I have never seen the book he refers to but the chapter headings mentioned by MacArthur are intriguing. They include; loyalty week, knock on every door week, how to have a pledge system, how to canvass a neighbourhood (for donations), how to motivate people to give, how to make them feel guilty and transfer their guilt into donations, etc! I suppose the most famous example of such coercion was the German fund raising campaign organised by Tetzel in 1517. Contributors were offered deliverance from years of suffering in purgatory, with the jingle:

> As soon as the coin in the coffer rings
> The soul from purgatory springs.

In 2 Corinthians 9:7 Paul adopts a rather different approach: 'Each of you should give what you have decided in your heart to give, not reluctantly or under compulsion, for God loves a cheerful giver.'

Paul's words give two clear principles. First: your giving is your decision. 'Each of you should give what you have decided in your heart to give.'

I have heard of certain churches where the leadership demands to know the financial circumstances of their members and the leaders then tell the people what they must give. Biblical giving is giving which is 'not under compulsion'. Second: our giving must not be reluctant. As we have said, it should be with a smile on the face, with a sense of privilege, and in grateful recognition of God's goodness to us.

The right mind

The Bible tells us that it is not enough to be *faithful* stewards; we must also be *wise* stewards. I have had personal experience of receiving a circular from a group presenting themselves as a charity, and giving to them, only to find them exposed in the newspapers a little later as a total fraud.

Wise stewardship means making your giving a matter for serious prayer but it also means using common sense. There are some things that you should obviously give to. I hope all readers of this book are committed members of a local church. If we enjoy the benefits of such a fellowship we will no doubt want to contribute towards the cost. But even if you are a committed church member you will want to ensure that the money given is used wisely by the church, and as a committed member you will have every right to make your views known.

Both Old and New Testaments teach that caring for God's servants who have been called to dedicate themselves full-time to God's service is the responsibility of God's people. To the priestly tribe, the Levites, God gave 'all the tithes in Israel as their inheritance in return for the work they do while serving in the tent of meeting' (Numbers 18:21). Paul says that those who preach the gospel should receive their living from the gospel (2 Corinthians 9:14). Today it is encouraging to see a renewed emphasis on the local church sending out workers and accepting responsibility for them. This is by no means yet a common principle and today there are thousands of Christian workers at home and abroad relying on our support.

Besides supporting individual workers, we shall want to give help to projects and organizations. Rather than trying to support too many of these it is probably best to concentrate on a few. Get to know these organizations, find out all you can about them, visit them if possible. Let your giving to these organizations be part of a real relationship with them.

There have been a number of scandals in recent years when charitable organizations have been found to be misusing the monies entrusted to them. Wise stewards want to be sure about organizations that they are committing monies to. How can we be sure? The in-depth relationship with a few organizations that I have just proposed is the best way. If you have any doubts about an organization then write to them: don't be afraid to ask questions. The organization's willingness to answer your questions and their openness in answering will probably tell you a lot about them.

There are some obvious questions that you can ask:

1. Is the organization audited annually by independent qualified accountants?
2. Are the audited figures made available to the general public?
3. Who are the board members and senior staff?
4. Does the organization have a council of reference and if so could they supply you with the names?
5. What percentage of total funds received is spent on administration and raising further funds?

Wise stewardship today must include the possibility of giving by deed of covenant. Information about this and related topics appear on pages 85–91.

The right price

Two examples we have already looked at have shown that the giving that honours God is sacrificial giving. Paul praised the Macedonian Christians because they gave 'as much as they were able and even beyond their ability' (2 Corinthians 8:3). The poor widow in the temple gave far less than the rich people who were giving at the same time, but Jesus said, 'They all gave out of their wealth; but she out of her poverty, put in everything — all she had to live on' (Mark 12:44).

A remarkable incident in the life of King David illustrates this truth. The prophet Gad had told David to 'build an altar on the threshing floor of Araunah the Jebusite'. Seeing the king approaching, Araunah bows low and asks why David has come. When David replies that he wants to buy Araunah's threshing floor so that he can build an altar to the Lord, Araunah responds by inviting him to 'take whatever pleases him . . . Araunah gives all this to the king.' David's answer teaches a vital principle of Christian life and service which can certainly be applied to our giving. 'The king replied to Araunah: No I insist on paying you for it. I will not sacrifice to the Lord my God burnt offerings that cost me nothing.' You may read the story in 2 Samuel 24: 18–24. The principle David states should govern every area of our lives as Christians. The symbol of our faith is a cross. When Isaac Watts surveyed that cross his response was:

> Were the whole realm of nature mine,
>   That were an offering far too small.
> Love so amazing so divine,
>   Demands my soul, my life, my all.

We are back to the joy of sacrifice. Cheerful sacrifice should be our manner of giving.

Chapter 8

God wants us rich!!!!

In chapter 6 I asked the question: 'When it comes to giving, what is in it for me?' Though I said I didn't like the question I replied that giving offers a great deal to the giver. I said the Christian giver cannot fail. A movement which is increasingly popular today seeks to build on these truths. Sadly the building they erect is grotesque; the movement has led many astray. The basic Scripture text of this 'prosperity movement' is 3 John 2. In the King James version this reads: 'Beloved, I wish above all things that thou mayest prosper and be in health even as thy soul prospereth.' From this and other Scriptures it is argued that material prosperity glorifies God. If Christians are not prospering then Satan is robbing them of their inheritance in Christ. A favourite statement is that 'we are the Kings Kid's and we should live like it'. It is the 'biggest and the best' that brings glory to God.

The secret of such prosperity sounds very simple. 'Give and it shall be given unto you' (Luke 6: 38). If you give to the Lord, he promises you a hundredfold return in this life (Mark 10:30). So invest in God and be prosperous for his glory. Fifteen million – dollar crystal cathedrals have been erected through the donations generated as a result of such teaching.

Like so much false teaching the prosperity message is a mixture of truth and error. Where do its advocates go wrong? First in their use of Scripture. This is wrong in two ways. First, it is highly selective. Scripture teaches that wealth is a zero value for the people of God. There are great dangers in wealth. Pause now, to read Luke 12:14–34 where Jesus points out some of those dangers. Similarly, Paul points out the dangers of riches in 1 Timothy 6:17, but he also says that those who use their riches well will 'lay up treasure for themselves as a firm foundation for the coming age' (v. 19). As for poverty, although it can be a curse it can also be a real blessing. It was to his disciples that Jesus said, 'Blessed are you who are poor, for yours is the kingdom of God' (Luke 6:20). They had left everything to follow him, now they relied entirely on him. Self – reliance is a constant danger for those who have ample resources, as Jesus' story of the rich farmer makes clear, but that was no longer a problem for these disciples. I appeal to those who teach 'prosperity' to stop coming to Scripture in search of verses to support their position but instead to look at Scripture as a whole and ask what it really says.

The second weakness in the way that 'prosperity' teachers use scripture is in the way they interpret the scriptures they select to support their position. Their basic text (3 John 2) is a perfect example. John Stott is only one of many commentators to point out that this is the 'everyday language of letter writing' at the time. The equivalent today would be a letter beginning, 'Dear Peter, I do hope that this letter finds you well.'

This is why the NIV translates the verse: 'Dear Friend, I pray that you may enjoy good health and that all may go well with you, even as your soul is getting along well.'

To use such a verse as a main foundation for the doctrine of material prosperity is to build on sand. The same can be said of another favourite verse of these teachers. In John 10:10 Jesus says, 'I am come that you may have life and live it to the full.' Those in the prosperity movement make much of the KJV translation of this 'life to the full' as 'abundant life'. They say it refers to material abundance. But to argue their position from this Scripture is once more to use the scriptures for their own ends. 'Life to the full is the eternal life of the kingdom with all its rich biblical imagery.' (Milne) 'The Greek word *perrison*, translated 'more abundantly' in the KJV means simply that believers are to enjoy this gift of life to the full. Material abundance is not implied either in the word 'life' or 'to the full'.

Furthermore such an idea is foreign to the context of John 10 as well as to the whole of the teaching of Jesus.'

A third problem about this teaching is that it — tragically — encourages a pagan view of possessions. A good way to understand that is to read Matthew 6:31–33 in *The Message*:

'What I'm trying to do here is get you to relax, to not be so preoccupied with *getting*, so you can respond to God's *giving*. People who don't know God and the way he works fuss over these things, but you know both God and how he works. Steep your life in God-reality, God-initiative, God-provisions. Don't worry about missing out. You'll find your everyday human concerns will be met.'

In 1 Timothy 6:6–10 Paul is teaching the right approach for Christians to material issues. It is interesting that what prompted this passage was false teachers who were 'selling' their teaching. Their activities led Paul to make his now famous statement, 'Godliness with contentment is great gain.'

The word translated 'contentment' means 'detachment or independence from things or possessions'. As I have already said, possessions are zero value for the believer. They have no lasting value and provide no eternal advantage. It is this eternal perspective which is at the root of our 'contentment' v. 7. 'For we brought nothing into the world, and we can take nothing out of it.'

People whose motive in life is to get rich are asking for trouble (v. 9). 'People who want to get rich fall into temptation and a trap and into many foolish and harmful desires that plunge people into ruin and destruction.' We have seen that later in this section Paul has encouraging things to say to those who are rich and use their riches well, but if the motive of your life is to get rich prepare for trouble! There is something about the drive to be rich that blurs the moral principles of believers.

The principle set out in Proverbs 30:8–9 is one we would do well to heed. 'Give me neither poverty nor riches, but give me only my daily bread. Otherwise I may have too much and disown you and say, "Who is the Lord?" Or I may become poor and steal, and so dishonour the name of God.'

A fourth criticism of this teaching is the way it affects our motive in giving. Danny Lehmann writes: 'Can you imagine being the Creator of the Universe and giver of life itself and having your children give to your work for the purpose of getting a return on what they give? Is this a child's love for his father? NO! It's pure selfishness and manipulation of God cloaked in Christian terms.' To give in order to get is the language of the world. We give for the glory of the one who has been so good to us.

Chapter 9

The Gift of Giving

Giving regularly, systematically and proportion-
ately is the will of God for every Christian. But do
some have a particular spiritual gift of giving? As
we have seen, Paul recognizes that the believers at
Corinth are excelling in certain spiritual gifts such
as faith, speech, and knowledge but he encourages
them to 'also excel in the grace of giving' (2
Corinthians 8:7). In Romans 12:8 he says, 'If a
man's gift is contributing to the needs of others,
let him give generously.' If we do not possess
particular spiritual gifts, we are still called to be
obedient to the commands of Scripture in those
particular areas of gifting. Even if we do not have

the gifts of the evangelist we are still called to
evangelize. With or without the gift of giving we
are called to be givers. Throughout the years of
church history God has called and gifted particular people to inherit or earn money and give it
intelligently so that his name is glorified and his
work enhanced. The ministry of Jesus and his
disciples was supported by several women with
means (Luke 8:3). Some have seen making money
and giving it, as their main calling in life, and I
believe that is a biblical position. Just as clearly as
God calls some to 'give up and go' he calls others
to 'stay and give'. To consider that one calling is
in any way more honourable than the other is, I
believe, wrong. John Wesley used to encourage his
people to (1) earn as much as they could so that
they could (2) save as much as they could in order
to (3) give as much as they could. I am sure that
most of us will be happy with his first two points
but what about the third?

As I reflect on this from the perspective of
missions I see a great need for many more to be
called to the ministry of giving. Romans 10:13–15
contains Paul's great mission statement: 'Everyone who calls on the name of the Lord will be
saved.' Then he sets out the logic of mission. He
asks four simple questions. 'How then can they

call on the one they have not believed in? How can they believe in the one of whom they have not heard? How can they hear without someone preaching to them? How can they preach unless they are sent? These four questions teach so much. First, the necessity to believe in Jesus Christ for salvation. In these days when the idea that there are many ways to God seems to increase in popularity it is important to go back to Paul's simple question. Second, that is essential that people should hear. The tragic reality is that two thousand years after Jesus gave us the commission to 'Go and tell' millions have still not heard. Thirdly, that the great priority in promoting mission is people, not methods, or plans. Fourthly, that people will never 'go' unless others 'send' them. Perhaps we should divide Christians into two categories when it comes to missions: those who go and those whose ministry in life is to send. There is much more involved in sending than providing the money, but without money no one will be sent!

In his booklet *Money Talks* Tom Rees reports a conversation he had with one of New Zealand's most successful business men, Robert Laidlaw. Laidlaw described a notebook he had preserved for many years. It had the following entries:

February 1st 1904. Age 18 years six months, wages £1 per week. I decided to start giving one tenth to the Lord.

February 12th 1906. Before money gets a grip on my heart, by the grace of God, I enter into the following pledge with the Lord that:

I will give ten per cent of all I earn up to £ . . .

If the Lord blesses me with £ . . . I will give fifteen per cent of all I earn.

If the Lord blesses me with £ . . . I will give twenty per cent of all I earn.

If the Lord blesses me with £ . . . I will give twenty five per cent of all I earn.

The Lord help me to keep this promise for Christ's sake; who gave all for me.

(A later entry reads:)

September 1910, aged 25. I have decided to change the above graduated scale and start now giving 50 per cent of all my earnings

Living by these principles Robert Laidlaw, through his gift of giving, made an immense contribution to the work of God around the world.

R.G. LeTourneau was American, a designer and manufacturer of earth-moving equipment. He said, 'I believe that God wants businessmen as well as preachers to be his servants, I believe that a factory can be dedicated to his service as well as a church.' Le Tourneau assigned over 90 per cent of his company's profits to the LeTourneau Foundation, the proceeds of which could be used 'only for the cause of Christ'. In the first five years the foundation gave almost $5 million to Christian ministries.

The biography of John Laing, whose (British) construction business achieved world-wide fame, shows how he arranged his giving at the age of thirty.

> Following a period of solemn prayer and dedication I drew upon a sheet of notepaper during September 1909 showing how I proposed to dispose of my income.
>
> If income £400 p.a. give £50, live on £150, save £200.
>
> If income £1,000 p.a. give £200, live on £300, save £500.
>
> If income £3,000 p.a. give £1,000, live on £500, save £1,500.
>
> If income £4,000 p.a. give £1,500, live on £500, save £2,000.

To this he added the proviso that, once the saving brought an interest of £500 per annum, he would live on £500, give away half of the remainder of his income and save the rest.

All over the world there are evidences of the impact of this man's gift of giving.

Some people who do not possess great resources also have a wonderful gift of giving. In my itinerant work I have stayed in homes all over the world with God's people who have the gift of giving. They give up their time, their privacy and their resources in order to serve me! I can tell you I often leave these homes truly humbled by the examples of selfless giving I have benefited from.

What I am describing is a *partnership*. It is what Paul had in mind when he thanked the Philippian church. 'I thank my God every time I remember you. In all my prayers for you, I always pray with joy because of your partnership in the gospel from the first day until now' (Philippians 1:3–5).

I pray for a new generation of Christians who see that they have been given the gift of giving and who take that gift and calling just as seriously as the missionaries and the ministers take their gifts.

Chapter 10

How Much should I Give?

Wouldn't everything be much easier if there could be a chart showing at a glance how much we should give in accordance with our income?

We have already seen that the simple answer to the question is *everything*. 'You were bought at a price' (1 Corinthians 6:20). But how much of that pay cheque does the Christian who recognizes the lordship of Christ actually give to the work of God? It is clear from scripture that what Christians give will vary and that it will differ at various times in our lives.

There are two important principles. First, our giving must be 'in keeping with our income'

(1 Corinthians 16:2). Paul encourages the Corinthian Christians to give to the Jerusalem believers 'according to what they have' (2 Corinthians 8:12). Many Christians feel that sermons and books on giving are not relevant to them because they have so little. 'I'm glad the preacher mentioned money and I hope the people who are well off will listen carefully.' But even if we have only a little, the subject of giving concerns us. If we have an income then we must give 'in keeping with that income'. I need to stress here that we can never start too early in this matter of giving. Let us teach our children to give as soon as income comes their way. Students, even if you feel survival on a grant is impossible, learn to give. If we don't learn when we have a little, and don't begin to plan our giving from that little, we will probably find it very difficult to change our habits when the income level increases. We need to remind ourselves again that the amount is not the issue, as we have seen in the example of the poor widow. But sometimes it is the wealthy who get upset. There are so many calls on their wealth. They get involved in a project and find themselves covering a very large portion of it. If you are wealthy don't be too surprised at feeling like this, because for all of us the giving is to be 'in keeping with the income'.

This leads to the second principle. It calls into question the title of this chapter. What we should be asking is not, 'How much should I give?' but 'How much should I keep?' A rich giver and a poor giver may *give* very different amounts but they also may *keep* very different amounts. I am sure the amount they choose to *keep* is the vital figure.

In seeking to answer the question we must recall principles we have already mentioned. Let us make the tithe our bottom line. The tithe 'belongs to the Lord'. Let us also be sure that our giving involves us in joyful sacrifice. C. S. Lewis would not talk about percentage giving. The only safe rule, he said, was 'to give more than we can spare'. 'Our charities should pinch and hamper us. If we live at the same level of affluence as other people who have our level of income, we are probably giving away too little.'

Ronald Sider suggests what he calls 'the graduated tithe' as a modest beginning to break the materialistic stranglehold in which many of us are held. He and his wife calculated honestly what they would need to live for a year. The standard they set for themselves was 'reasonable comfort but not all the luxuries'. A more radical approach, he suggests, would be to use the national poverty level as the base amount. Then, for every additional thousand dollars of income above that basic amount they decided to increase their giving by five percent on that thousand so that of the first thousand on top of their base amount they gave fifteen percent, the second twenty percent and so on. This was definitely planned giving 'according to their income'. Nevertheless Sider suggests that 'the proposal is probably so modest that it verges on unfaithfulness to Paul's principles in 2 Corinthians, although it is also sufficiently radical that its implementation would revolutionize the ministry and life of the church'. The truth is that no chart can be given to show how much we should give. But we should be clear about these principles:

1) Don't rob God. Remember the tithe, we can't afford not to give it.

2) Our giving will be 'in keeping with our income'.

3) Whatever our income, 'our charities should pinch and hamper us'.

However, let me emphasize again that we must not be thinking only of the giving of money. I believe a crucial question for all of us is — what standard of living do I choose? I have seen many

Christians who find that in order to maintain their chosen standard of living they have to work incredible hours, that both partners in the home must be in work, and in such circumstance, it is easy for the giving to suffer. Not only the giving of money but their giving of time to God, the family, church, people. Christians often complain about the pressures they experience, they express concern that they are not spending their time in the right way, but the possibility of making radical choices concerning their chosen standard of living does not appear to be considered. It's a vital question for every Christian. What standard of living will enable me to be most effective as a worshipper and servant of God?

Chapter 11

The Witness of Giving

Donald Hay, Fellow and Tutor in Economics at Jesus College, Oxford, writes: 'It is I believe, one of the greatest failings of the church today that the consumption patterns of Christians apparently differ so little from those of unbelievers around them. There could be no better indication to our materialistic neighbours that our faith means very little to us than that there should be no difference in the very area to which our materialistic society is dedicated—the accumulation of possessions.'

This is one reason why the prosperity movement can be so damaging. Instead of offering a radical alternative to this materialistic message it offers a 'spiritual' materialism.

Jesus, by contrast, rejected 'the accumulation of possessions'. He made it clear that our attitude should be one of relaxation and that we should have different priorities. Matthew 6:25–27 shows how different our attitude should be. We are not to worry about such things as what we eat, drink, wear and so on. Life, says Jesus, is more important than these things. Our heavenly Father looks after the birds of the air without them spending time storing in barns. Will he not look after his people?

Simon Webley points out the difference that there should be in our attitude to possessions:

> The world asks how much we own, Christ asks how we use it. The world thinks more of getting, Christ thinks more of giving. The world asks what we give, Christ asks how we give, the former thinks of the amount, the latter the motive. To the world money is a means of gratification; to the Christian, a means of grace, to the one an opportunity of comfort; to the other an opportunity for consecration.

When Paul encouraged the Corinthians to send their gifts to the Jerusalem believers he pointed out that such obedience would be a powerful witness. 'This service that you perform is not only supplying the needs of God's people but is also overflowing in many expressions of thanks to God. Because of the service by which you have proved yourselves, people will praise God for the obedience that accompanies your confession of the gospel of Christ, and for your generosity in sharing with them and everyone else' (2 Corinthians 9:12–13). It is 'the obedience that accompanies our confession' that will speak to people. Such actions of sacrificial giving done with no thought of personal gain but for God's glory add weight to the words of Christian witness.

I have seen this happen in situations where emergency relief has been required in times of crisis. People who for many years have had no time for the message or even for the missionary adopt a completely different attitude when they have seen the missionary sacrificing to meet their needs in the emergency. I have also witnessed the same on an English housing estate where there had been much witness with no evident result until a small team began doing gardening and shopping for the elderly. If practical 'acts of obedience accompany our confession' our witness is greatly enhanced.

Another vital area of witness in connection with giving is the way Christians deal with the money

they are given. Paul was very concerned about this
in connection with the gift from the Corinthian
churches. 'We want to avoid any criticism of the
way we administer this liberal gift. For we are
taking pains to do what is right not only in the
eyes of the Lord but also in the eyes of others' (2
Corinthians 8:20,21). Notice two things here.
First: Paul takes great care about this matter. The
gift has not yet been received but Paul is already
taking pains to ensure that it is correctly adminis-
tered. Second: Paul is concerned that what is done
must not only be right but must be seen to be right.

The attitude, 'let people think what they please.
I know before God what I am doing is right', is
not acceptable. Sadly, over the years, and certainly
in recent years, the church has been hit with too
many scandals in connection with the administration of funds. These scandals could have been
avoided if there had been the commitment to
glorify God in this area that Paul displays. Please
notice the responsibility of the church treasurer or
the Christian organization's accountant in making sure that God's name is glorified. It is not only
the evangelist in the organization who is involved
in witness. A few days before I wrote this section
I returned from visiting an area of our O.M.
ministry that had been almost torn apart with

problems in this area. Suspicions had led to gossip and that gossip had even spread into the local community, undoubtedly harming the witness. When we investigated the allegations the reality proved to be not embezzlement but inadequate accounting records and a lack of accountability in handling funds.

What we as Christians do with the resources God gives us is certainly one of the most vital areas of our witness as we approach the end of this millenium. As we saw earlier in 2 Corinthians 8, the Macedonian churches were a challenging example. How could they live as they did? It was 'through the grace God has given the Macedonian churches' (v. 1). Only the grace of God can enable us to live aright in this, as in every other area of our lives. Left to ourselves we will have the wrong priorities and make the wrong choices.

How did this grace of God work in those Macedonian Christians? The opening verses of 2 Corinthians 8 show that it did two things for them. It enabled them to give the right amount and to give it in the right way. The amount was sacrificial and the motive was God's glory. Such giving from us will have a similar impact as their giving had in its day. God was glorified, the givers were blessed, critical needs were met and there was a powerful witness to the authenticity of the Christian faith. Let us pray that many more of us will make a similar response to the grace of God in our lives!

TAX MATTERS —
some practical aspects of giving

1 Deeds of Covenant

Anyone who pays UK Income Tax should consider making use of a Deed of Covenant in order to maximise their giving. By this means you can increase significantly the value of your gifts. This is because a Church or Charity can claim back from the Inland Revenue tax at the Basic Rate on the 'grossed up' value of the payment made.

For example, assuming a Basic Rate of tax of 23%, for every £77 which you covenant (i.e. the amount which you actually pay over) the Registered Charity or Church can claim back £23 from the Inland Revenue. Therefore, your £77 gift is worth £100.

A Covenant must be for a period capable of exceeding three years, so that the most popular term is four years. Should you die before the covenant expires, no liability will fall upon your estate since the deed is automatically cancelled by death.

To enter into a Deed of Covenant, you need to complete and sign a simple form in the presence of a witness (two witnesses are required in Scotland). These forms are usually available from your Church or Registered Charity. However, an example of a Deed is set out at the end of this Appendix.

Tax relief is usually given to you at your top rate of tax. You deduct and retain Basic Rate income tax when you make the covenanted payment. The extra relief due to you if you are liable for Higher Rate tax will be given when you settle your Higher Rate liability or by repayment.

If you are not liable to tax at the Basic Rate, or you are paying tax only at the Lower Rate, then the use of such Covenants will probably be inappropriate.

By way of example, in the current tax year 1997/98, if you are a Higher Rate taxpayer, for every £77 which you donate under a covenant, the Charity will be able to claim back £23 in tax and your own tax bill will be reduced by a further £17.

Entering into a Deed of Covenant with a particular Church or Charity for a period of four years or more may not be appropriate in your circumstances. However, this does not prevent you from taking advantage of Covenant Schemes. For instance, the Charities Aid Foundation provides a covenant service for individuals and companies whereby you can enter into a Covenant with the Foundation and can ask them to send the gross value of your gifts to individual Churches, Charities and Missionaries of your choice. For more information contact:- The Charities Aid Foundation, King Hill, West Malling, Kent, ME19 4TA. (Telephone 01732-520000).

2 Deposited Covenants

It is possible for you to give a Charity the benefit of an immediate lump sum while retaining the tax advantage of Covenants by means of a 'Deposited Covenant'. In effect there are two transactions:-

(a) An interest free loan repayable in four equal instalments and

(b) A Deed of Covenant for four annual payments, the net amount of each covenanted payment being equal to one quarter of the loan.

The annual loan repayments cover the amount due under the Covenant. It is essential that the initial loan must not be made before the tax payer makes the Deed of Covenant.

The Charity benefits because not only does it have the use of the money at the outset, it also is able to reclaim tax each year on the covenanted payments.

3 Gift Aid

If you want to make a single gift to a Church or Charity of £250 or more, the payment can be treated in the same way as a Charitable Covenant, i.e. Basic Rate tax is regarded as having been deducted, and Higher Rate relief is given where appropriate. You will be required to give the Charity a certificate (R. 190 (SD)) to enable the charity to reclaim the tax.

4 Payroll deduction schemes — Give as you earn

If your employer is participating in the above scheme, you can authorize them to deduct up to £1,200 from your earnings before tax, for passing on to charities, chosen by you through charity agencies with which your employer has made arrangements. In this way you receive full tax relief for the contributions made.

5 Inheritance tax

All gifts to charity are exempt whether you make them in your lifetime, on death or out of a discretionary trust.

6 Capital gains tax

If you make a gift of an asset to a Charity, no Capital Gains Tax (CGT) is payable, nor will an allowable loss arise.

For instance, if you own shares on which you would realize a taxable gain if you sold them, you would not have to pay the tax if the shares were given to a Charity. This leaves the Charity free to keep the shares as an investment or sell them tax free if it needs the cash.

7 Your will

If you wish to leave some or all of your Estate (your assets less liabilities) to a Church or Charity, then it is essential to make a will. You cannot assume that your relatives or friends will carry out your wishes unless you have made a valid will. A will simply gives instructions as to how your estate is to be distributed when you die. It is advisable to obtain sound legal advice concerning the preparation of your will to ensure that your wishes are made clear and unambiguous.

DEED OF COVENANT

I, ...   Please indicate
of ....   Mr/Mrs/Miss
....   etc your full
....   names
....
.............................Post Code ....

undertake to pay   each year for   The actual
four years (or during my lifetime if shorter)   ANNUAL
from today the sum that will, after   amount you
deduction of income tax at basic rate be   wish to give

£..

Signed, sealed and delivered by

Date ....   is in joint
Witness's signature ....   names both
....   partners
Witness's address ....   must sign
....

Second witness (in Scotland only)

Witness's signature ....
Witness's address ....
....